the Never... book

by GRAHAM HARROP

ISBN: 978-0-9683227-4-1

never...

WASH YOUR SNEAKERS IN CEMENT

never...

never...

never...

never...

never...

HIDE A WALRUS IN YOUR FRIDGE

never...

SHOWER IN BLUEBERRY JUICE

never...

never...

Sleep WITH AN eLepHANT

never...

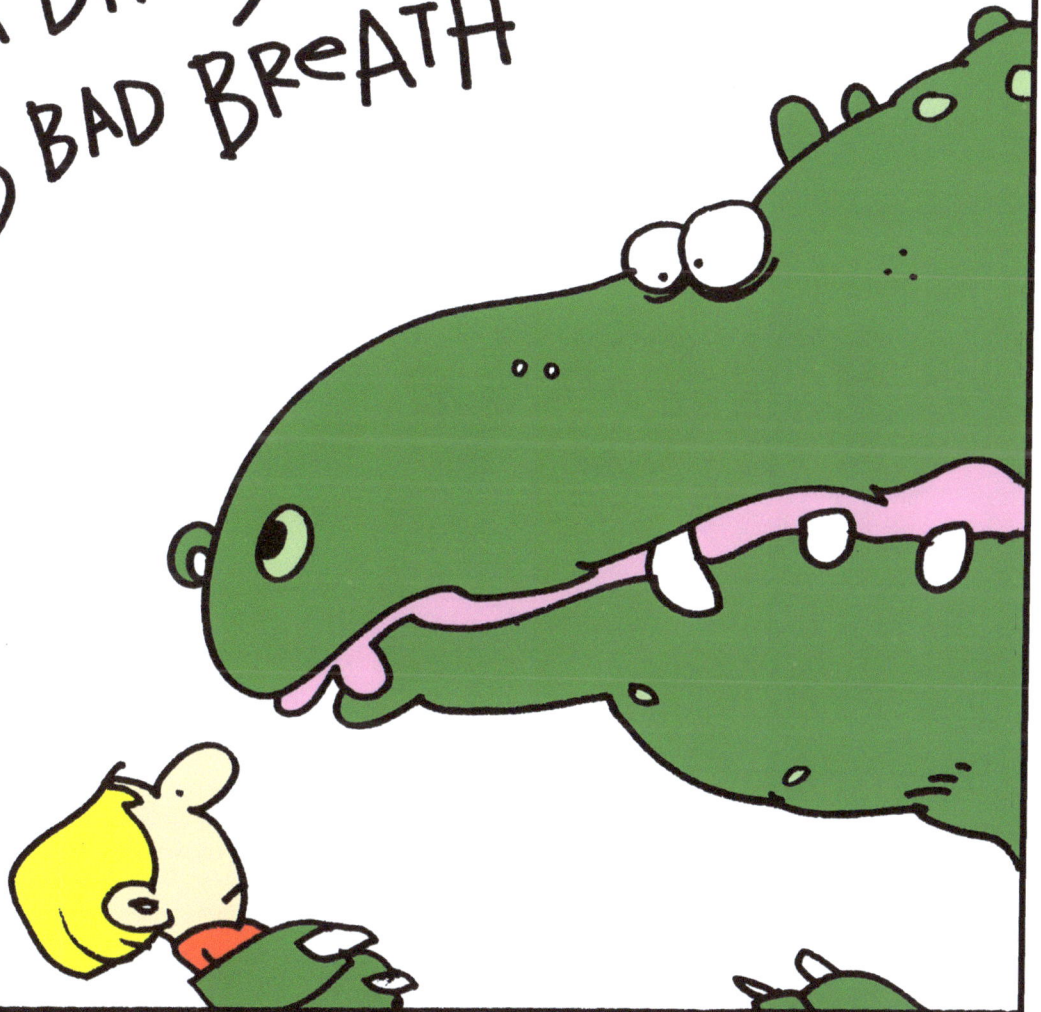

TELL A DINOSAUR HE HAS BAD BREATH

never...

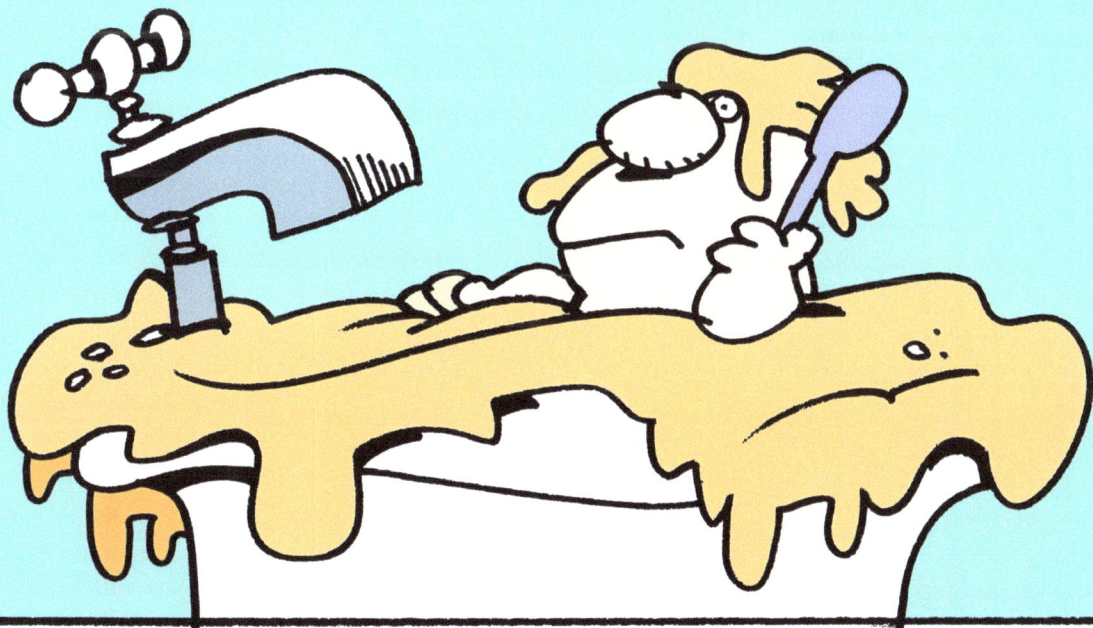

never...

never...

never...

never...

never...

TEACH YOUR DOG TO FLY...

Gryndstone & Fusspot Press

www.ingramcontent.com/pod-product-compliance
Lightning Source LLC
Chambersburg PA
CBHW042105040426
42448CB00002B/144

9780968322741